MARBLES

MARBLES

New and Collected Poems

Laura K. Deal

Published by First Church of Metaphor

First Church of Metaphor Poetry Collections Vol. 1

Copyright Laura K. Deal 2014

ISBN-13: **978-0692219928**

ISBN-10: **0692219927**

Cover Photo by Laura K. Deal

Cover Assistance by Janet Fogg

Dedication

For all the poets, dreamers, and metaphorians in my life, with special thanks to my Dream Camp family for welcoming my poetry into our circle and helping me remember who I am.

Contents

The Dreamtime Lost and Found

In the Dreamtime Lost and Found
there's a bubble-gum pink piggy bank
with three quarters inside. I glimpsed it there,
and it was mine, but somehow I didn't take it.
I hope the Dreamtime Lost and Found
has the journal my daughter lost in my dream,
the story of herself, slipping away in the airport
on her way home from college.

I expect the Dreamtime Lost and Found is
full of classrooms...
all the classrooms I can never find
when I need to take the test
I didn't know I had in the
class I didn't know I'd signed up for.
Maybe those other rooms, that show up
unexpectedly in a corner of a house
behind a hidden door, maybe those
are the lost classrooms, transformed.

The Dreamtime Lost and Found
might still have my virginity,
but since I stopped looking for it
a few years after I lost it,
they probably tossed it long ago.
I do hope they kept my lost dreams though;
both the aspirations I had for myself
and the sleeping visions that slithered away
before I could catch them
in my net of words.

Does the Dreamtime Lost and Found
have the map that shows
how I got from Chang Dung to
Chong Cheng in only four months?
Did I ride the i-Ching?

But what I really wonder is
if the Dreamtime Lost and Found
ever had the door out of the locker room—
the cement block locker room
at the end of all the long halls
where the Man chased me when I was a little girl.
He's going to kill me, or cut me up,
at least I know he has a knife,
and please, oh please, where is that door?

Run, little girl! Hurry!
Run until you're trapped
and the only way out is to
Wake Up!

Remembering how to breathe—
that's what matters. Being awake
doesn't shake the fear from my bones.
This earthquake of a dream
crumbled the foundations of my world
night beyond night,
saturating my childhood.

But at Dream Camp, things happen.
I'm pretty sure the
Dreamtime Lost and Found
hangs around the edges
waiting for a chance to toss
a long-forgotten memory into the circle.
A blue shoe. A scar. A man.
What better place to take a quiet moment
to close my eyes, and re-enter
the long cement halls.
The Man, chasing me.
But this isn't a dream,
and I'm no longer five,
so I imagine myself stopping.
Turning. Facing him for the
first time. Asking, "What do you want?"

I can't really see his face
but I can see what he holds, and
it's not a knife.
It's a golden sphere, a ball of light.
He holds it out to me.
"I have come to return
Your authentic self to you."

Oh, little girl. How could you have known
that the Man in our nightmares
was working for the Dreamtime Lost and Found
all along?

Light in the Woods

Within the sad wood of my heart
walk the fabled children
searching for adventure in their quest
to find their way home.

My heart holds the secret house
of the clever old witch
who lures the children in
so that she might
sweeten the pot with the fat
of their young, unlived lives,
and consume them, to live a little longer
in this precious and bitter world.

In the woods of my heart
also lives Vasilisa's doll,
helping the children
go lightly down that wooded path,
carrying Vasilisa's lamp in a pudgy hand,
candlelight shining from the skull's eyes.

Yes, the woods hold shadows
underneath their arching limbs
but the children walk on,
drawn by the light from the dawn
of the universe, deeper into
what I know of myself.

Mother's Day 2014

On this cold, wet, snowy Mother's Day,
my daughters study for their final exams,
taking their education seriously,
with the background awareness
that not everyone on the planet
shares this privilege. I hold them
in gratitude and pride, for the ways they've
blossomed because of, and despite,
my quirks and foibles as a human mom.

Next to this joy in my heart, the grievous shadow
of hundreds of Nigerian schoolgirls stolen
from their school to be kept and sold into slavery,
their mothers shocked and grieving.
Sweet innocence, taken by the devil,
girls targeted because of their desire
to learn, to grow their own power in the world
through thought and education.

Heartbroken mothers, terrified daughters,
and all I can do is add my voice
to the demand that someone save them.
My outrage is necessary, but never enough.
What else can I do from my side of the world?

I carry those girls and their families
in my praising, grieving heart as I
venture out into wet spring snow
to shake the first few inches
from the tarps covering the garden,
the ones my husband and I draped
over tomato cages and secured with clothespins,
to protect the tender buds and slender stalks
of my iris and peonies, because
the weight of Gaia's weeping could easily break them,
and the freeze might nip their potential beauty
in the bud.

I'd Thought There'd Be Angels

These are the dreams I'm left with:
The long, slow, sinister dreams
where shadows loom and
monsters lurk in dark back yards
and people shit on the ground
and then feed their babies in the filth.

I'd thought there'd be angels
or birds, or at least some bright color
to show I'd stepped the right step,
walked my path with conviction,
if not courage. Loved the unlovable.

But the celebrations of dreams
are more ephemeral than the
fierce lessons; like the man with the knife
who laughs as I try to call 9-1-1
on a broken phone that never had
a nine to begin with. I'm left to find
my own solution, to face my own
death over and over until I have
no name, no wallet, no body.
Just my own wounded spirit
trying to hold onto the light
from the star where I was born,
trying to see the perfect round
wholeness of myself in the splinters
of a shattered mirror. The pain
of those sharp edges never rests,
never lets me get complacent,
but always opens new dark corners
in the homeless hotel of my psyche,
inviting me to pull back the cobwebs
I've used to poultice my wounds,
urging me to hold my broken
heart out to the world to offer love
again. And again. And again.

Well, perhaps I exaggerate. There was an
angel once, in the depths of a cave,
though a moment before it had been
a decaying corpse. Once, decades ago,
that angel spoke to me of
comfort and hope and life
eternal, beyond the physical.
In my doubt, I summon him
again to my imagination, and
he's still there, a towering being of light
as real as any memory from
waking life. With the shattered mirror
of my heart I catch
the pale reflection of his glory
and beg forgiveness for my belief
that I am alone in this.

Dream Mother

For Billie Ortiz

After the dark dream
when the image lingers like an answer
whose question is forgotten
in the stark light of day
the dreamer needs her sisters
those who can speak of blood
and the fragile wings
of hope in one breath,
those who know
a woman's secrets.

After the wild dream
of running naked in
the street, the classroom, and the office,
the cloak of the dreamer
is the only clothing that suits,
the fabric of projection
bunching and smoothing
the wrinkled edges of awareness.

After the terrifying dream
of storms and floods
and drowning
the dreamer needs her clan
a family birthed from dreams
nurtured by the dream mother
who holds us in her awareness
and gentles our fevered fears.

After the glorious dreams
of celebration, of awareness expanded,
the dreamer wants only
to sit with those who understand
whose hearts are open
whose blood-lines matter less
than their dream-lines,
who find their family
where dreams gather together
and speak.

Gusts

All my intricate plans
collapse like a house of cards
in a Chinook wind, scattering
to earth and sky.
Parts of the scaffolding end up
in Kansas, where placid cows
taste the oddness of my thought
and move on to greener pastures.

I wander in the back yard,
turning over the six of diamonds,
the queen of spades,
the three of clubs,
and wonder if my routines
merit the intrigue of puzzling out
how to rebuild them, or if it's time
to stop structuring my thoughts
out of something as flimsy,
as ephemeral, as fate.

Where do poems go when they die?

Do they wander bardo realms
of mixed metaphors
and marauding word hoards?
Do they fragment into haikus?
Or reincarnate into fund-raising pleas,
their next life destined
for the junk mail?
Or do they go to heaven,
to be recited lovingly,
movingly, by wise angels
for the pleasure of the
Holy Poet?

Dreamer's Notes

This is not a race for winning,
the old woman said,
It is only for the doing,
the care along the way.

The old woman said,
If you could see from here
the care along the way
is the greatest gift of all.

If you could see from here,
you'd know that open-hearted courage
is the greatest gift of all
when you stand upon the bridge.

You'd know that open-hearted courage
is all that gets you through
when you stand upon the bridge
of irreconcilable paradox.

Is all that gets you through
your profound appreciation
of irreconcilable paradox?
Life needs love, and sacrifice.

Your profound appreciation
reveals the gifts that you are given.
Life needs love, and sacrifice.
The hardest challenge

reveals the gifts that you are given.
Don't take my word;
the hardest challenge
is learning for yourself.

Don't take my word;
your task here
is learning for yourself,
asking all the questions.

Your task here,
when you walk among the living,
asking all the questions—
it's walking into mystery.

When you walk among the living
it is only for the doing,
it's walking into mystery.
This is not a race for winning.

Crisis

Into this heart
I pour an epoxy of words
the stories that tell themselves
grasping for meaning
when there is none
just the long labyrinth
into death. Every turning
a change, joyous or
grievous it hardly matters
there is only reaching
for the light dark
and the yearning to
grasp paradox as tightly
as I hold your
lifeless hand.

Crybaby

Do you see what I have here?
A diamond of pain,
Crushed to cutting strength
By sheer determination.
The fierce drive to survive.
Do you see what light the diamond holds?
The light of my gift
My divine sunshine
My blessed weeping
Trying to soothe the fierce
Winds of the family.
Do you see me inside there?
The intense vibration
Of energy received,
The divine pulse too loud,
Too stressed.
Torqued.
See me.
Spin the diamond.

Pantoum for a Ghost

Don't hover beside me.
I saw you die
I wept at your bedside
Your breath evaporated.

I saw you die
Not a moment, a movement.
Your breath evaporated,
Your living ceased.

Not a moment, a movement,
That step to oblivion.
Your living ceased—
You believed you would.

That step to oblivion
A false promise
You believed you would
Stop. Like a clock.

A false promise,
This hope of escape.
Stop, like a clock?
A delusional dream.

This hope of escape
Lost forever,
A delusional dream
Your spirit must walk in.

Lost, forever,
Not knowing you've died,
Your spirit must walk in
A remembrance of living.

Not knowing you've died
You cling to my grieving
A remembrance of living.
I bless you. Move on.

You cling to my grieving—
I wept at your beside.
I bless you. Move on.
Don't hover beside me.

Imaginary Barrier

It looks like a brick wall
the kind you'd have to scale
in boot camp.
The kind I look at and
say, "No way."

But here's the secret
I'm still learning:
It isn't made of brick,
or stone, or even glass.
It's built of boxes.
Boxes I've put myself in
boxes other people put me in
boxes full of miscellaneous crap
I've gathered since childhood.

Like the idea that if it's hard
It's too hard
Or that rejection means
my writing's
not good enough
not marketable
not the right genre.
The thing is,
the stories I tell on paper
are the ones I need to hear.

I saw that wall of boxes
in a dream, the gaps between
revealing a lion penned within,
a huge cat,
full of instinct
and secret ways of knowing.
Those boxes can't cage the cat.
Not anymore.

I pull one out,
sort through the crap inside,
keep only the little yellow lantern
I once took to summer camp.
Because all it needs is a new battery
or a photovoltaic cell
to bring me the light of the sun,
and then I'll be able
to see my way
as I throw out the rest
and free the lion.

House

The house has fallen to its knees
its walls soaked heavy
with the words of the family,
whispering them in the night,
insinuating through an inner ear.
Words laden with scents of
lilacs, burned hamburgers,
tears, and candle smoke.

Punkin tastes the dry attic dust
that clings like cobweb to her fingers,
coating all the once-bright colors
of life's impedimentia
in uniform pale gray.

Punkin lived here when she was new,
in the once-new house
in the young western town.
The house will never fall,
will always be red brick
and white wood, will always
struggle to hold itself together
even as its family drifts away
to other states, other planes.

When the basement flooded,
the family scrambled to save
the words and clutter of ancestors
long gone, clinging,
as the house clings,
to memories and whispers
and laughter, but not the tears.
Not the flood.

Punkin can't touch the walls
because they've just been painted,
or was that thirty years ago?
The cool kiss of maternal love
pillows against the bedroom wall,
trying to absorb Punkin's tears.
The clothes dryer cheerfully wakes itself,
dings, and falls back into eager waiting.
The house chuckles
at some secret irony of its own.

Punkin, she hears those creaky whispers
as she memorizes her populated ceiling,
in her room where she'll always
have the lazy summer afternoon
to wander in daydream.

En boca cerrada no entran moscas,
and the dark flies of truth can't escape.
The entryway snarls at the grit coming in
as the house wipes the dust
from its knees.

The Path

The rain makes a sound
that pulls me out of a dream
of roads flooded by the sudden wash
from clouds so sodden they fall apart
hiding the moon and every star.
I'm left adrift, without a map.

When I was younger, I had a map,
though I allowed my voice no sound.
I hoped one day I'd be a star,
but no one else believed my dream,
so I let it go and break apart
like a love note forgotten, lost in the wash.

But it doesn't all come out in the wash
and youth only rarely follows a map.
I had to fit in while soul stood apart,
the anguish inside a subliminal sound,
the sound of a heart that clings to a dream
and wishes the same wish on every star.

I began to search: I wore a star,
sought purification in the wash,
dug for meaning in every dream,
begged the sages for a map,
sought the sacred in chanted sound,
tried to keep ego and awareness apart.

I woke to the truth that we're not apart,
but the light in our eyes is the stuff of a star.
The spirit spoke, with or without sound,
a voice in my head when I sorted the wash,
a nudge in my gut to ignore the map,
a pull in my heart to pursue my dream.

I fled from death once in a dream
but stopped myself. And from a part
that remained aware, that had a map,
I saw death transformed into a star
and stood in loving light that washed
through me and left me whole and sound.

Again I dream of being a star
that soars apart, above the muddy wash
and a charts a new map with my own sound.

Just Jump

Jump into the river of the tears of God
There's no point swimming
Just let the water carry you
Far beyond your understanding
To places where the desolation
Gives way to something green
Where the sobbing of the Earth
Meets the rending of the Sky
And your grief becomes endurable
In comparison to the river's current.
Just jump, because the stepping stones
Were long since swept downstream
And the bridges only rainbows
And hope confined to dreams.
Just jump, and when you wash up
On some strange bank by a pool
Climb out and see if you know
Who stares back at you from below.

Missed Understanding

This dance of electrons
reflecting emotion
a funhouse mirror
from one perspective.

Reflecting emotion
of well-worn patterns,
from one perspective
I see betrayal.

Well-worn patterns
retreat into dark.
I see betrayal,
slide into self-pity,

retreat into dark
and sleepless nights.
Slide into self-pity,
dream of blood

and sleepless nights.
You try to make light.
I dream of blood.
I weep in private.

You try to make light.
I slowly respond.
I weep in private.
You offer apology.

I slowly respond,
this dance of electrons
You offer apology,
A funhouse mirror.

The End of the World

You remember the day
the world ended.
The day your mother
sat down across from you,
her red drinking glass
held like a shield
against your judgment
as she placed the tab
of LSD on her tongue,
her first communion
with a new, uncertain god.

The day the world ended
she let down
her spindly hair, preening
as if she wore long feathers.
She chirped like a bird
then sang a lullaby you
hadn't heard since
your ears were small enough
to be constantly hurting
and you remember the pain
of hearing her cry and
you wish, you wish
that she'd saved some
sweet release for you,
to numb the edge
of the world.

The day the world ended
she wanted to drive
fast and crazy on Highway 6,
going anywhere, everywhere, nowhere
and you took the keys,
buckled her in,
and drove into the sunset.

You pretended that the signs
were unclear, that there'd be
another day to say
all the things...
Desperate, you tried to say them,
but Mother was one with the onrushing scenery
and your words flowed out the window
into an eddy
where they tumbled into the shoulder
and piled up among
empty water bottles, used condoms,
and dirty diapers.

The day the world ended
you took your mother home
tucked her into your own bed
with her imaginary better half,
that part of her who'd never
spanked you
belittled you
gotten sick.
You sat beside her
until sleep finally took her
and you saw her as she
must have been before
life got her drunk and
rolled her for change:
sweet, unlined, and
still on speaking terms with hope.
You kissed her forehead
and tiptoed out.

It was easier than bearing witness
to the end of the world.

Complicity

The intruder lifts the window
slides in, silent as a dream
unpacks his ex's boxes,
offers sweet poison to the guests.
We protest, we do not want to die,
but the syrup's swallowed,
the deed complete.
All that's left is to arrange
ourselves. How do we
want to be found?
Eyes open, to see what's coming,
on the other side of oblivion.

My First Contrary Thought

I should have control of my own brainchild.
It should have a sympathetic guardian,
not one who shudders at its
awkward angles and tangled hair.
It should mature while spirits deepen
and make its outlandish declaration
for those who will linger in wonder
and chant the echo of its incantation.

The Dogs Bark

They come by twos at first:
the eyes of the Mothership
watching, sampling,
listening to everything we say.
The gunmetal saucers
sneak in behind the clouds
so we never know if they're there.
Collectively, we pretend they aren't,
we say the pictures are Photoshopped,
the videos are fakes.
But the dogs know.
The dogs bark.
That's how it starts.

Next comes the black triangle,
a ship so silent
we never see it in the sky
until its shadow slides over our skin.
It moves too slowly
or too fast
and we tell ourselves
it's the military,
not of alien origin.
As if that's a comfort.

The day they gas us
we can no longer pretend
as our lungs refuse to
understand oxygen,
and our skin
turns the color of
cooked asparagus.
Finally, in the face of
the common enemy
we all look alike,
gasping, dying fauna
of a useful planet.

We have enough breath
to see the Mothership
eclipse the sun.

Earthquakes

I walk with heavy stride, carrying earthquakes
In every step, my current incarnation
Formed with grandiose attempts to harmonize humanity.
Before me, the unconscious, an oceanfront expanse,
My old beliefs behind me in a marvelous heap.
At times the pot at the end of the rainbow is psychedelic,
And I wear the garb of roaming artisan
Peddling my wares to dozens of gravestones,
The occupants responding with visceral growls.
And I still harbor ridiculous train-building fantasies,
Praying that my intentional splash will be hallowed.

Dream Garden

When you dig
What do you find?
The roots of life
Piercing the soil.

What do you find
In the roots of your soul,
Piercing the soil,
Seeking crevices in bedrock?

In the roots of your soul
Where the hurting lurks
Seeking crevices in bedrock
Holding on.

Where the hurting lurks,
There the truth lies
Holding on
To the shadow's gift.

There the truth lies.
There you open
To the shadow's gift
With a willing heart.

There you open
The roots of life
With a willing heart
When you dig.

Raceless

I am a woman of no color.
Culturally descended
from oppressors who enslaved,
massacred,
stole the land.
Yet my forefathers lived
poor farmers,
pacifists,
teachers.
My foremothers struggled
to survive,
stay sane,
raise good children.

I am a woman of no color.
But I am not white
like clouds
or snow.
My skin contrasts with paper,
my brown hair grays.
I bleed red.

Just as good men are twisted
by awkward strictures of patriarchy,
my good intentions are twisted
by cultural definition of skin.

I am a woman of no color,
yet my personal shade changes
and shifts with the season.

In my dream, labels fade
like last decade's tan;
skin doesn't define self.
I see in your eyes
Spirit kin to my Spirit,
eyes of different colors
greeting siblings.

But when I wake,
I am a woman
of no color.

Some Days

The most challenging of all art forms
is the navigation of disquieting intimacy
when the world of possibility
stands on the edge
of an unprecedented,
holy-shit-that's-high cliff,
and even the combined wisdom of
international heads can do nothing
that doesn't feel haunted.
In those moments, even with
the miraculous cooling of rainwater,
you just know
you're going to be late for work.

Never Wear High Heels

Except once, when you're twenty,
and the world pulses
in time with your heart
and all lead singers
have names like Danny
and are too cute for words,
and maybe, if you wear
those red spikes and
that red dress
and catch a little buzz
you'll dance into
such a groove
that the world will
fall in love with you.

Liquid

We begin nearly liquid,
thin walls of cells
demarking our limits,
the body still fluid enough
for soul slipping in,
testing, examining boundaries.
Stuck.

Once born, the wall of skin
toughens, abraded by air,
by light, by touch,
silky groin tested
by diapers, wipes, powders.

Then knees, elbows, hands,
first skin abandoned,
replaced by pads of callus and scar.
Trying to grow a shell
against a sharp, rough world.

Soft creases harden,
cracks and crevices
carry memories of sun,
of passion.
Laughter, tears, rage
Shellac us.

The body grows tree-like:
rough bark, stiff limbs,
until the soul no longer
swims, but stagnates.

And finally, breaks
liquid free.

Here is Where

Here is where I step out
alone
seeming unafraid
into the spotlights
of my dream.
Out of reach of anyone
who might help
guide me,
into the glare
and blink
of what I thought.
Here is where I step.

Road Trip

Pulse beat
road trip
sunrise
light on waving grain
birds startled
flock flying
soaring
wings beat
across road
soaring
gone
up to speed.

Road sweeps
beneath tires
empty horizons
cloudless blue.

Sunrise hot
behind us
bright day
light hearts
fingers drum the wheel
miles pass
sweet communion
of silence
life behind
life ahead
deep joy.

My heart's wings
beating with tears
can't hold this day
with you
going west
going on.

Little town
sleepy folk
sunny sidewalk
breeze through.

Stop at the water
sunlight scattered
seeking itself
on wind-blown waves
birds land
pool light into bands
air, water, light, love.

Your hand in mine.

Mom's Chore

Rarely, yearly, by some magic
she would open the oven
beyond its usual limit
laying the door down flat
against the cupboards below.

Seated on her swivel stool,
hands encased in yellow
Playtex gloves, armed
with brush and Easy Off
she painted.
Not portraits, or landscapes
but long steady rows
of caustic paste that
abraded my nose unlike
any other smell ever
to dwell in the oven.

Her patience, uncomplaining,
astonishes me now,
though then it was only
one of the odd rituals
of adulthood, another reason
not to grow up.

After an hour,
the smell permeating the house,
the baked-on black
of daily dinner splatters
turned to goo, to be
dragged away on a paper
towel, brown sludge on white,
on yellow gloves
on my memory.

Inside the oven,
clean speckled gray walls,
smooth tracks for shelves,
all evidence of past
unpleasantness wiped clean.

Memories

The ones that stick
get sticky. Laden
with resonance, enriched
with meaning. Like dreams,
I ask, "Why this one, now?"
The fear of the burglar,
the childish abuses,
returning to school after illness,
the question, "Do you want out of it?"
They wake me up and chime
for my attention,
old familiars whispering,
"Remember me?"
I pass them through my awareness
like prayer beads.

Child's Destiny

Hidden beneath the trivia
    of present detail
Sleep the child's dreams
    of future generalities.

The child knew
    as if told by the future self
The secrets of my destiny
    my duty to myself.

Now that I have begun
    to listen
The child reawakens
    whispering her secrets.

From future to past
    the dreams were revealed
And from past to future
    they are remembered.

The circle of destiny
    the path of myself
Childlike dreaming forming
    the me that is waiting.

Marbles

I went a little crazy
in my twenties
as so many of us do,
losing our marbles as we
try to navigate the world
before the great kaleidoscope
shift of Saturn's return.

My particular brand
of craziness grew
out of the riptide of life
where two great currents met:

The first, the powerful vibration
of ancestral experience.
Women in my line
going back three generations
met their husbands in college,
and women before them
married even younger.

That giant wave of tradition
crashed against the rising tide
of women reclaiming their own lives
women who saw their mothers
subsume their creative energies
into the few socially acceptable channels
of teaching
housework
motherhood
and taking care.
And the daughters said
No. Not I. I'll be liberated
from all that.

The riptide took me under.
I nearly drowned,
trying to find my own way
living on nothing wages
the future utterly unpredictable.
My relationships couldn't bear
the weight of ancestral expectation.
My mom, bless her heart,
sent a clipping
when I was twenty-six:
A study had shown
that women were far
less likely to marry
after the age of
twenty-six.
That's it, time's up.

Thank the universe for
shifting kaleidoscopes.
At twenty-eight the riptide ebbed.
In the light of Saturn's return,
I met the man I'd marry,
the one who loved me
despite my backpack
full of crazy.

Good fortune blessed us.
We bought a little house.
We dug a garden—
the first I'd ever owned.
As I spaded the soil,
extracted the roots of
tenacious weeds,
small treasures appeared.
A child's rainbow of spheres:
Marbles.
Green, yellow, red, blue, white.

The metaphor was undeniable.
In my marriage,
I found my marbles.
In the safety of "us,"
I found myself.
And just in time.
The next wave washed
me into motherhood.

But raising my children
was not my only calling.
Words and stories
clamored to get out onto paper.
Into the world.
Even as we moved
to a bigger house,
a bigger garden,
by letting out words,
I managed the weight of
my backpack of crazy.

Planets revolved around the sun.
I wrote. I helped my children
learn to navigate the world,
and watched in awestruck love
as they blossomed.

They grow up.
The kaleidoscope shifts.
My empty nest looms
right there on the horizon,
in the arms of Saturn
as he marks his second orbit
since my birth.
Suddenly, writing is not enough.
Wild ideas arise.
I lead with my heart
and discover a new calling.

I hold its possibilities in mind
and dig in my garden,
this garden I've worked for
seventeen years,
this soil that's yielded
beans and berries,
squash and potatoes,
and two toy trucks.
As I dig and consider
this possible new path
I turn up a marble.
The silvery, mirrored surface
gives me a wide-angle
view of myself. And when
I hold it to the light
it glows heart green
and whispers,
"Yes."

Notes

"Mom's Chore" was originally published on *MiseEnPoem.blogspot.com* on January 26, 2009, Don Kingfisher Campbell, Editor

"The Dreamtime Lost and Found" appeared in *Collective 2014*, Kayla Bowen, Editor-in-Chief

The following poems were originally published on *FirstChurchofMetaphor.org:*
"The Dreamtime Lost and Found"
"Mother's Day 2014"
"Dream Mother"
"Crybaby"
"Earthquakes"
"Dream Garden"
"Never Wear High Heels"
"Mom's Chore"

The following poems were originally published in *Dreams from the Word Hoard*, available as an ebook at Smashwords.com:
"Where do poems go when they die?"
"Dreamer's Notes"
"Dream Garden"

About the Author

Laura K. Deal revels in metaphor wherever she can find it, especially in dreams, poems, and stories. She's the founder and editor of FirstChurchofMetaphor.org, and the author of *The Newcomer's Guide to the Invisible Realm: A Journey through Dreams, Metaphor, and Imagination.* Many of the poems in this collection were inspired by dreams. Others arose in Laura's poetry and writing workshops using words and phrases drawn at random. She calls this creative dance with chance *Juxtaprise.*

www.ingramcontent.com/pod-product-compliance
Lightning Source LLC
Chambersburg PA
CBHW020952030426
42339CB00004B/59